My First Bibl

The Story of th

Kathy Lee and Roma Bishop

Little
EAGLE

One day, Jesus came to a town.
A crowd of people gathered round him.
'Tell us a story,' said one.
And everyone was quiet.

Jesus sat down
and began to speak.

3

'There was once a man
who had a hundred sheep.
He knew them all by name,
and he took good care of them.

4

He found juicy green grass for them to eat,
and he guarded them against wild animals,
because lions and bears prowled round about.

5

At night the shepherd brought them safely home.
Each night he counted his sheep
as they went in through the gate
to make sure they were all there.

But one night, instead of a hundred sheep,
there were only ninety-nine.
One sheep was missing.

The sheep had wandered away
from all the others, and now it was lost.
It was alone in the darkness,
a long way from home.

"I must find it," the shepherd said.
So he left the other sheep safe in the fold,
took a lantern and went out into the night.

9

The shepherd walked and walked,
listening for the cry of a lost sheep.
At last he heard it, faint and far away.

When the shepherd found the sheep,
it was so tired it could hardly stand up.
So he picked it up gently and carried it home.

When he got home, the shepherd was so happy that he invited all his friends to a party.

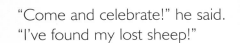

"Come and celebrate!" he said.
"I've found my lost sheep!"

13

When Jesus had finished the story,
he looked at the crowd and said,
'Sometimes people do bad things.
They go away from God, just like that sheep
who went away from the shepherd.

'But God still loves them.
He wants to find them again,
and when he does,
he is as happy as the shepherd
who found his lost sheep.'

This story can be found
in the Bible in Luke 15:1-7

Published in the UK by Eagle Publishing
PO Box 530, Guildford, Surrey GU2 4FH
ISBN 0 86347 506 X

First edition 2002

Copyright © 2002 AD Publishing Services Ltd
1 Churchgates, The Wilderness, Berkhamsted, Herts HP4 2UB
Text copyright © 2002 Kathy Lee
Illustrations copyright © 2002 Roma Bishop

Printed and bound in Malta